Mom & Dad—I Promise I'll Get into College

Perspectives from a High School Student
and Her Dad

Lexi Shavitz and Jeff Shavitz

THiNK*aha*®

An Actionable Child/Parent Journal

E-mail: info@thinkaha.com
20660 Stevens Creek Blvd., Suite 210
Cupertino, CA 95014

Published by THiNKaha®
20660 Stevens Creek Blvd., Suite 210, Cupertino, CA 95014
http://thinkaha.com
E-mail: info@thinkaha.com

First Printing: September 2016
Paperback ISBN: 978-1-61699-189-0   1-61699-189-5
eBook ISBN: 978-1-61699-188-3   1-61699-188-7
Place of Publication: Silicon Valley, California, USA
Paperback Library of Congress Number: 2016942474

Dedication

This is dedicated to all parents and their children who experience the exciting, frustrating, and stressful college application process. It is our intention that these AHAs will share different reflection points from the perspectives of both the parent and the child. Good luck with your application process for getting into college.

Acknowledgement

Dad—I had a great time writing this book with you. As the younger daughter, I know you already experienced the college process with Jen. And now it's my turn. Thanks for being a great dad, and I'll miss you when I'm at college!

Lexi—I can't believe you are already starting the college application process. To use the cliché, "the time has gone by so fast." When you were a child, I always loved going to your tennis matches and dance recitals and doing the typical "dad-stuff" with you. Writing a book together has been an incredible experience to share with you. I love being your dad! Congratulations on writing your first book!

Although you are the best author in the family, I want to also acknowledge Jen and Andrew; Mom and I could not be more proud of our three special children!

How to Read a THiNKaha® Book
A Note from the Publisher

The THiNKaha series is the CliffsNotes of the 21st century. The value of these books is that they are contextual in nature. Although the actual words won't change, their meaning will change every time you read one as your context will change. Experience your own "AHA!" moments ("AHAmessages™") with a THiNKaha book; AHAmessages are looked at as "actionable" moments—think of a specific project you're working on, an event, a sales deal, a personal issue, etc. and see how the AHAmessages in this book can inspire your own AHAmessages, something that you can specifically act on. Here's how to read one of these books and have it work for you:

1. Read a THiNKaha book (these slim and handy books should only take about 15–20 minutes of your time!) and write down one to three actionable items you thought of while reading it. Each journal-style THiNKaha book is equipped with space for you to write down your notes and thoughts underneath each AHAmessage.

2. Mark your calendar to re-read this book again in 30 days.

3. Repeat step #1 and write down one to three more AHAmessages that grab you this time. I guarantee that they will be different than the first time. BTW: this is also a great time to reflect on the actions taken from the last set of AHAmessages you wrote down.

After reading a THiNKaha book, writing down your AHAmessages, re-reading it, and writing down more AHAmessages, you'll begin to see how these books contextually apply to you. THiNKaha books advocate for continuous, lifelong learning. They will help you transform your AHAs into actionable items with tangible results until you no longer have to say "AHA!" to these moments—they'll become part of your daily practice as you continue to grow and learn.

As the Chief Instigator of AHAs at THiNKaha, I definitely practice what I preach. I read *Alexisms* and *Ted Rubin on How to Look People in the Eye Digitally*, and one new book once a month and take away two to three different action items from each of them every time. Please e-mail me your AHAs today!

Mitchell Levy
publisher@thinkaha.com

THiNKaha®

Contents

Section I

Lexi's Perspective:
It's Hard Being a High School Student

Lexi Shavitz is a junior in high school (sixteen years old) and is a middle child with both an older sister in college and a younger brother. This section contains the pain and perspective she feels about the pressure of college.

1

My parents put so much stress on me to do well in high school. What about yours? @LexiShavitz

_____

_____

_____

2

My parents always bug me to join extracurricular activities. How many are you in? Is it enough for your parents? @LexiShavitz

_____

_____

_____

3

Everyone has their dream college,
but not everyone gets into it.
Don't panic! @LexiShavitz

_____

_____

_____

4

My teachers put so much stress about my
grades. Is it the same for you? @LexiShavitz

_____

_____

_____

5

My sister is so smart, which puts extra anxiety on me. Do you have siblings you are compared to? @LexiShavitz

_____

_____

_____

6

I'm trying to make the tennis team. It will
look good on my high school transcript.
Is there a team sport for you? @LexiShavitz

_____

_____

_____

7

I want to go to the University of Michigan,
but I don't think my grades are high
enough. Trying not to worry. @LexiShavitz

_____

_____

_____

8

I love my older sister and younger brother, but I'm trying to find my own identity in this crazy world. How about you? @LexiShavitz

_____

_____

_____

9

I became involved in Student Government and became secretary of my class. It's worth exploring. @LexiShavitz

_____

_____

_____

10

I try to study as hard as possible. This was not true freshman year, but I'm working much harder now. It's truly important.
@LexiShavitz

_____

_____

_____

11

I hate getting up at 6:30AM for school. I usually fall back asleep until my parents wake me up again. You do this?
@LexiShavitz

_____

_____

_____

12

Time flies. I can't believe high school will be over in 2 years. Use the time wisely. @LexiShavitz

_____

_____

_____

13

College life seems like so much fun. I love visiting my sister in ccllege. Can't wait. How about you? @LexiShavitz

_____

_____

_____

14

School, tennis, homework, friends — very difficult to balance. It's hard being a high school student. @LexiShavitz

_____

_____

_____

15

There are nights I just can't fall asleep,
thinking about the stress of getting into
college. Try not to panic. @LexiShavitz

_____

_____

_____

16

I feel the pressure to get straight A's (which I don't get). Not everyone is a straight A student. @LexiShavitz

_____

_____

_____

17

College is only 2 years away, which scares me on many levels. What about you?
@LexiShavitz

_____

_____

_____

18

The SAT and ACT are extremely frightening for me. Do you know anyone who's excited about taking them?
@LexiShavitz

_____

_____

_____

19

It's scary to start to plan out my SAT and ACT tutoring for these important exams. @LexiShavitz

---

20

I don't know how I'm going to sit through a full-day exam. I have a hard time focusing for that many hours. @LexiShavitz

---

21

A lot of my friends are very smart, which makes me work harder.
Hint: Make smart friends.
@LexiShavitz

_____

_____

_____

22

Like me, my friends want to attend good universities. Surround yourself with friends who want good things. @LexiShavitz

_____

_____

_____

23

Listening to music & watching TV is a
stress reliever for me. I also text my friends
non-stop when I'm stressed out.
@LexiShavitz

_____

_____

_____

24

Along with my academics, I love playing
tennis and watching sports. How about you?
@LexiShavitz

_____

_____

_____

25

I love my friends. I feel so lucky to have an amazing bunch of both girls and guys to hang out with. @LexiShavitz

_____

_____

_____

26

My parents and I did fight freshman year when they knew I wasn't working as hard as I could. How about you? @LexiShavitz

_____

_____

_____

27

I know how lucky I am to have really cool, loving parents. And I should tell them more often how much I appreciate them. @LexiShavitz

_____

_____

_____

28

My sister is my role model. I want to be like her. We're different yet the same, if you know what I mean. @LexiShavitz

_____

_____

_____

29

I hate when my teachers compare me to my older sister, who's one of the top students in her grade. "Why can't you be like her?"
@LexiShavitz

_____

_____

_____

30

My younger brother is a little stud. All my friends love him. Do you love your siblings? @LexiShavitz

_____

_____

_____

31

High school sports is so competitive.
I wish we had a jr. varsity tennis team,
but I'm trying hard to make varsity this year.
@LexiShavitz

_____

_____

_____

32

My parents made me visit a special guidance counselor to understand why I wasn't working harder. I went. Didn't help.
@LexiShavitz

_____

_____

_____

33

My friends all go to different schools (private, public, Jewish, Christian, in-home, etc.). So many types of high schools!
@LexiShavitz

_____

_____

_____

34

Until my sophomore year, I had never visited a college or university. I had no idea what to expect. @LexiShavitz

_____

_____

_____

35

There is so much pressure in my house,
school, and neighborhood to get into a
good college. You feel it as well?
@LexiShavitz

_____

_____

_____

36

I know my parents want what's best for me,
but it's sometimes hard for me to see it.
@LexiShavitz

_____

_____

_____

Section II

Dad's Perspective:
We Just Want What's Best for Her

It's hard as a parent to toe the line between saying "what to do" and helping our kids figure out "what's right for them." The section covers some good rules of thumb and advice parents should adhere to.

37

I just want my daughter and all of my children to be happy. That's it. @JeffShavitz

_____

_____

_____

38

Say this to your kids: You are not your brother or your sister — just be who you are. You're an amazing person. @JeffShavitz

_____

_____

_____

39

Does it really matter if you attend college X or college Y? Probably not, just do your best. @JeffShavitz

_____

_____

_____

40

Please know that "we love you very much," even though at times, you may not believe it. Hint: Don't forget to say this. @JeffShavitz

_____

_____

_____

41

I only wish my daughter knew that we honestly didn't compare her to her siblings. @JeffShavitz

_____

_____

_____

42

All of our friends talk about the insane amount of pressure put on children today. Is it the same in your family? @JeffShavitz

_____

_____

_____

43

Why do all of our children have to be so programmed with after-school activities? We are guilty as charged. @JeffShavitz

_____

_____

_____

44

As parents, we just want what's best for our children. Then why do we push them into situations that are not good for them? @JeffShavitz

_____

_____

_____

45

My 11-year-old is a great basketball player. I tell him to get a scholarship to save us some money. Only joking. ;) @JeffShavitz

_____

_____

_____

46

Let's encourage our children to get involved in extracurricular activities and develop real relationships with teachers. @JeffShavitz

_____

_____

_____

47

What will my daughter want to major in? Hard for a young person to make that decision while being so young. @JeffShavitz

_____

_____

_____

48

As a parent, I hope she is very careful with dating, sex, etc. We need to discuss openly these issues with our children. @JeffShavitz

---

49

Acknowledge your children's accomplishments. Take nothing for granted. @JeffShavitz

---

50

Expand your horizons. Take a course on cooking or art or something new to really learn about life. @JeffShavitz

_____

_____

_____

51

Strange thinking of my 2nd child off to college in a few years. I know it sounds trite, but years are flying by. @JeffShavitz

_____

_____

_____

52

As a parent, I love having social media (FB, texting, Instagram) to constantly stay in touch. @JeffShavitz

_____

_____

_____

53

Parents need more therapy than their children going through the college process. Do you recognize this? @JeffShavitz

_____

_____

_____

54

It would be cool if my daughter joined the same sorority as my wife's. (I don't care, but my wife asked me to include this.)
@JeffShavitz

_____

_____

_____

55

What a difference in my daughter from freshman to sophomore year! She is really trying, and it's showing! #ProudParents @JeffShavitz

_____

_____

_____

56

It's hard when your child gets sick and they are thousands of miles away. @JeffShavitz

_____

_____

_____

57

Be honest as a parent. Are you pushing your child to a specific school to appease your ego? Be honest. Don't. @JeffShavitz

_____

_____

_____

58

We have to catch ourselves when we compare any of our children to each other. It's not fair to them. It's not fair to us. @JeffShavitz

_____

_____

_____

59

I hate the pressure on all these children. Why can't they just enjoy their childhood years? @JeffShavitz

_____

_____

_____

60

I encourage my children to really get involved at school. It's such an amazing opportunity that needs to be explored.
@JeffShavitz

61

It's scary to think about the drugs, alcohol, and sex issues that are prevalent now with high school and college students.
@JeffShavitz

62

How would you feel if your child wanted to drop out of college because it wasn't right for them? @JeffShavitz

_____

_____

_____

63

My wife is on the board of our high school.
It doesn't hurt getting to know the school
administrators on a personal level.
@JeffShavitz

_____

_____

_____

64

My job is to help my children discover their
passion, whatever it may be. @JeffShavitz

_____

_____

_____

65

It's hard to admit, but we need to let our children be their own selves and do what's best for them. Hard to do, right?
@JeffShavitz

_____

_____

_____

66

I never ever want my daughter or any of our children to lose touch with us. It's easy when they live under your roof.
@JeffShavitz

_____

_____

_____

67

As a parent, I just hope we instilled the right value system so she does the right thing in college. @JeffShavitz

_____

_____

_____

68

Thank you for being the best daughter.
I will truly miss you when you're away.
@JeffShavitz

_____

_____

_____

69

One of my greatest joys for Lexi is that she surrounds herself with great friends who have a similar value system to hers.
@JeffShavitz

_____

_____

_____

Section III: Lexi's Perspective

Section III

Lexi's Perspective
of the College Application Process

It's crazy to think about how fast time is flying and how soon I'll be applying for and leaving to college. #DontPanic. This section looks at some of my thoughts surrounding the application process and choosing the right school.

70

Colleges like to see original people.
Am I being original enough?
@LexiShavitz

_____

_____

_____

71

Although only a sophomore, I'm working on developing my college resume now. Are you? #BePrepared @LexiShavitz

_____

_____

_____

72

One of my friends is doing very poorly in school. He is telling us he doesn't want to attend college. It's a shame. @LexiShavitz

_____

_____

_____

73

This summer, I visited my cousins at Penn State University to get a feel for being on a college campus. Amazingly fun! @LexiShavitz

_____

_____

_____

74

I visited the University of Michigan to see
my sister. I love big schools with lots of
school spirit! @LexiShavitz

_____

_____

_____

75

I can't believe how many colleges there
are. I have no idea how I'm going to narrow
down the choice to a select few.
@LexiShavitz

_____

_____

_____

76

I hope I stay in touch with my high school friends when I start college. @LexiShavitz

_____

_____

_____

77

My publisher, Mitchell Levy, suggests that I go to a big school with a large alumni where I might want to live when I work.
@LexiShavitz

_____

_____

_____

78

There are good guidance counselors that will help me choose my "Safety," "Target" & "Reach" schools. I will use them.
@LexiShavitz

_____

_____

_____

79

Florida (my state) has a special "pre-paid" program that makes it more affordable for students to attend a public university.
@LexiShavitz

_____

_____

_____

80

I hope to attend a college outside of Florida. I love Florida, but I want to experience something different. @LexiShavitz

_____

_____

_____

81

I need to start meeting with my guidance counselor soon to understand my options for college. Is it too early? @LexiShavitz

_____

_____

_____

82

I didn't work hard during freshman year but now see how important doing your best is. I'm #Committed now. @LexiShavitz

_____

_____

_____

83

My sister's friends tell me it's important to
get into a good school so I develop great
friends for the rest of my life. @LexiShavitz

_____

_____

_____

84

I do think a lot about the excitement I
will feel when I get accepted into college.
@LexiShavitz

_____

_____

_____

85

Is everyone really applying to the same
5-10 schools in my grade? I hope not.
How do I compare? @LexiShavitz

_____

_____

_____

86

I know deep down, there is a college for
everyone. What are you thinking about?
@LexiShavitz

_____

_____

_____

87

Sophomore year is going by so quickly.
I'm writing this book over Christmas break.
@LexiShavitz

_____

_____

_____

88

In sophomore year of high school, teachers already talk about college, which can be so irritating. @LexiShavitz

_____

_____

_____

89

I really do want to do my best. I can honestly say that now. I didn't feel this way during freshman year. @LexiShavitz

_____

_____

_____

90

Staying after school for extra help with my teachers does help. My parents forced me to go, now I like it. @LexiShavitz

_____

_____

_____

91

I'm no good at standardized testing, but I am going to try really hard. How about you? #StandardizedTestsSuck @LexiShavitz

_____

_____

_____

92

Grades matter. My parents used to tell me to work hard in 3rd grade. I now know those grades don't matter at all for college.
@LexiShavitz

_____

_____

_____

93

It's hard being the middle child, especially when my sister did so well in high school and got into a great university.
@LexiShavitz

_____

_____

_____

94

Many of my older, really smart friends
are getting rejected from their first choices.
It's so competitive. #DontPanic
@LexiShavitz

95

I want to be a sports broadcaster. I love watching all sports & I understand a lot about most professional and college sports.
@LexiShavitz

_____

_____

_____

96

Since I know I want to be a sport broadcaster, I now need to figure out the best school I should/could go to.
@LexiShavitz

_____

_____

_____

97

My dad went to Tufts University, my mom
Emory University. They're small schools.
I want a big fun school w/ good academics.
@LexiShavitz

_____

_____

_____

98

I'm going to miss my 2 dogs when I go to college. What will you be leaving behind?
@LexiShavitz

_____

_____

_____

99

I think about my brother, Andrew, who will be alone with my parents when I go off to college. @LexiShavitz

_____

_____

_____

100

I know I'm fortunate to attend sleep-away camp. I hope some of my camp friends will go to the same college as me. @LexiShavitz

_____

_____

_____

101

I'm already thinking about who I want to room with during my freshman year of college. Too much? @LexiShavitz

_____

_____

_____

Section IV

Dad's Perspective of the College Application Process

This is an exciting and scary time for a parent. We want the best for our child, but we don't want to pay too much money and don't want our kids to move too far from home. In reality, we really want the best for our kids, whatever they decide to do. This section covers thoughts parents have at this time in our children's lives.

102

Is it too early to start tutoring my child for college when they are born? The answer is yes. Parents can be crazy. @JeffShavitz

_____

_____

_____

103

I don't remember getting into college being so competitive when we applied 30 years ago. @JeffShavitz

_____

_____

_____

104

Who ever knew about the big business of private college guidance counselors?
Sign me up. @JeffShavitz

_____

_____

_____

105

I'm going to spend so much money getting her tutors for the ACT. It better work.
Is there a money-back guarantee?
@JeffShavitz

_____

_____

_____

106

A tutor for $500 per hour for her ACT and SAT? Are you joking? @JeffShavitz

_____

_____

_____

107

I'm happy to pay for tutors, but you better study hard. @JeffShavitz

_____

_____

_____

108

What a difference 1 point makes on the ACT! Is a 29 a lot less than a 30? My daughter is going nuts waiting for her score. @JeffShavitz

_____

_____

_____

109

My oldest daughter studied until the wee hours & overslept for her SATs and had to take it a few months later. Who does that? @JeffShavitz

_____

_____

_____

110

My wife & I will never travel again on the day of the ACT/SAT, to make sure our child is up and has a good breakfast. @JeffShavitz

_____

_____

_____

111

I didn't have a college adviser in high school, and I turned out okay. @JeffShavitz

_____

_____

_____

112

Please apply to #Tufts & #Emory. We gave
so much money over the years, thinking you
may be interested in our alma mater.
@JeffShavitz

_____

_____

_____

113

There are lots of great universities,
but Harvard, Yale, Princeton, Stanford,
and others do sound better than the masses.
@JeffShavitz

_____

_____

_____

114

The college essay — I hope she can think of something creative to write about. @JeffShavitz

_____

_____

_____

115

Tell the truth, did you write your college essay for your child, proof it, and make the words less sophisticated? @JeffShavitz

_____

_____

_____

116

It's a privilege to attend any university, especially a private university. @JeffShavitz

_____

_____

_____

117

College is so expensive. It's crazy.
@JeffShavitz

_____

_____

_____

118

If you go to public school, I'll buy you the
greatest gift of your life, like the down
payment of your house! @JeffShavitz

_____

_____

_____

119

Moving my oldest daughter into college was nuts. I have never spent so much money at @BedBathBeyond in my life! @JeffShavitz

_____

_____

_____

120

Start saving young for college. I'm not a financial adviser, but it's more money than you can imagine. @JeffShavitz

_____

_____

_____

121

Tuition is one expense that I planned for. How about flights, clothes, sorority dues, parents' weekend? It doesn't stop! @JeffShavitz

_____

_____

_____

122

We didn't have Uber in our day. I can't believe how many rides my oldest takes back and forth to classes. @JeffShavitz

_____

_____

_____

123

Do you know the difference between a 529 Plan and other college savings plans? Learn, b/c saving is critical. @JeffShavitz

_____

_____

_____

124

Amazing but true how most of our friends'
children are applying to exactly the same
schools. @JeffShavitz

_____

_____

_____

125

Deep down as parents, do you go nuts when you hear that all of your children's friends are applying to the same school?
@JeffShavitz

_____

_____

_____

126

Parents try to one-up their friends with which school their child attends. It does sound cool to say my son is at Harvard!
@JeffShavitz

_____

_____

_____

127

I did Tufts alumni interviewing for many years. I'm beyond impressed with the accomplishments of these young people.
@JeffShavitz

_____

_____

_____

128

The competition is fierce. I would never be accepted to Tufts if I were applying today.
@JeffShavitz

_____

_____

_____

129

It's painful when you see your child, niece, or nephew not get into their first choice. @JeffShavitz

_____

_____

_____

130

How many of your college friends are you still in touch with? For me, it's 3 that I'm still very close with. @JeffShavitz

_____

_____

_____

131

Do you feel a sense of pride and camaraderie with your school? @JeffShavitz

_____

_____

_____

132

If you could do it all over again, would you still attend the university you attended? Why or why not? @JeffShavitz

_____

_____

_____

133

I'm not sure why I always refer to college as "college" vs. "university." Is it just me?
@JeffShavitz

_____

_____

_____

134

Is it really a good idea to room with your best friend from high school? I don't think so. @JeffShavitz

_____

_____

_____

135

I'm scared to have my child attend college out of state, because who knows if they will ever come back. @JeffShavitz

_____

_____

_____

136

Visiting colleges and taking their tours was very special and fun father-daughter bonding. Don't miss out! @JeffShavitz

_____

_____

_____

137

My wife & I spent semesters in London. I highly recommend that your child spends a semester someplace else in the world. @JeffShavitz

_____

_____

_____

138

College is a lot more than learning out of a textbook. My wife and I believe this 100%! @JeffShavitz

_____

_____

_____

139

College is fun, but please study hard so you
get the most out of these 4 years.
@JeffShavitz

_____

_____

_____

140

Can it really be that I graduated almost
30 years ago? Now I feel old. @JeffShavitz

_____

_____

_____

What Are Your AHAs?

Thanks for reading *Mom & Dad—I Promise I'll Get into College*!

Got any "AHAmessages" that would fit with this book?

We'd love for you to share them!

Tweet us **@happyabout** and/or **@JeffShavitz** and **@LexiShavitz**, and tag it with **#AhaMe**.

About the Authors

Lexi Shavitz is a junior in high school and has an older sister, Jennifer, attending the University of Michigan and a younger brother, Andrew, in grammar school.

Lexi, having watched Jen just a few years earlier go through the college application process, had the idea of collaborating with her dad to write a book about "getting into college."

Lexi loves being involved in various school activities to help her school become a better environment for the students, both academically and socially. She partakes in the school's "leadership organization" and has been a class officer in the student government so she can interact with the faculty as much as possible to help improve school spirit and represent the student body. Her true passion is the friendships she has built over the years through school, as well as the friends she has made in summer camp for the past ten years. She also enjoys playing tennis and working out in the gym.

She has spent the past three years working every weekend with special needs children and has been involved with the Israeli Tennis Centers Foundation, which helps less fortunate "at risk" children in Israel learn life skills and become educated, all while enjoying the sport of tennis.

Lexi enjoys watching all sports and currently is interested in majoring in journalism and eventually pursuing a career in sports broadcasting after college.

Jeff Shavitz is a successful entrepreneur whose passion and purpose for creating "his life" was the driving force behind leaving his lucrative position with Lehman Brothers to enter the world of entrepreneurship. After successfully selling his payment processing company, Jeff started TrafficJamming, a virtual membership group comprised of different business services created for independent business owners and entrepreneurs to help grow their companies.

Author of four other books, including number-one Amazon-bestseller *Size Doesn't Matter—Why Small Business Is BIG Business*, Jeff actively participates in business, civic, and philanthropic organizations, including the Young Presidents' Organization.

He graduated from Tufts University and spent one semester at the London School of Economics. He is married with three children, and besides family, health, and world peace, his selfish goal is to play the 100 top golf courses in the world! To learn more about Jeff and his business, visit www.trafficjamming.com.

AHAthat™

AHAthat makes it easy to share, author, and promote content. There are over 30,000 quotes (AHAmessages™) by thought leaders from around the world that you can share in seconds for free.

For those that want to author their own book, we have time-tested proven processes that allow you to write your AHAbook™ of 140 digestible, bite-sized morsels in 8 hours or less. Once your content is on AHAthat, you have a customized url that you can use to have your fans/advocates share your content and help grow your network.

Sign up for a free account to start sharing content today: http://AHAthat.com

Want to quickly be an author to demonstrate your expertise? Start authoring your AHAbook at http://AHAthat.com/author

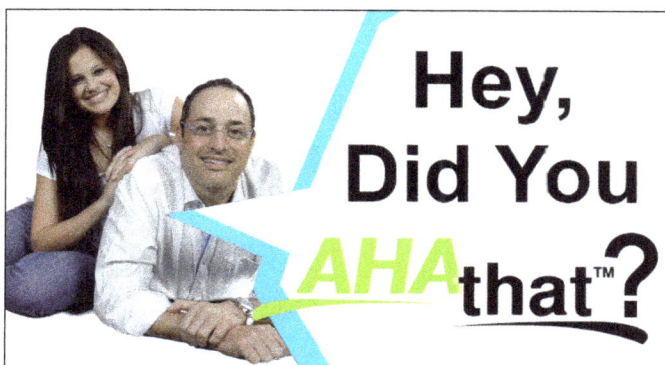

Please pick up a copy of this book in AHAthat and share each AHAmessage socially at http://aha.pub/gettingintocollege.

www.ingramcontent.com/pod-product-compliance
Lightning Source LLC
Chambersburg PA
CBHW070541080426
42453CB00029B/808